Butterflies & Skin

Dirty Sweet Poetry

Tiffany Simone

Creative Talents Unleashed

GENERAL INFORMATION

Butterflies & Skin

Dirty Sweet Poetry

By

Tiffany Simone

1st Edition: 2017

This Publishing is protected under Copyright Law as a "Collection". All rights for all submissions are retained by the Individual Author and or Artist. No part of this publishing may be Reproduced, Transferred in any manner without the prior **WRITTEN CONSENT** of the "Material Owner" or its Representative Creative Talents Unleashed.

www.ctupublishinggroup.com

Publisher Information
1st Edition: Creative Talents Unleashed
info@ctupublishinggroup.com

ISBN-13: 978-1-945791-28-4 (Creative Talents Unleashed)
ISBN-10: 1-945791-28-4

Credits

Amazon Description

Brenda-Lee Ranta

Book Cover

Mitch Green

Editor

Sarah Lamar King

Foreword

N.R. Hart

Dedication

To MK

For waking me up.

foreword

In this remarkably passionate collection of poetic musings, Tiffany Simone takes us on a thrilling roller coaster ride of emotions; ranging from love, desire, romance, lust, despair, hope, vulnerability, and everything in-between.

She is a master at getting to the core of your emotions in such a way that she is inside your head rummaging around in your feelings. She weaves your innermost thoughts into her decadent and sensual poetry, filling you with sensations of *love*, *longing*, and *passion*.

Simone's words provide comfort for the hopeless romantic in you, knowing you are not alone in your feelings. Her words are beautifully heartfelt, and transform the ordinary into sheer magic!

N.R. Hart, Author of *Poetry and Pearls*

Table of Contents

Table of Contents

Table of Contents

Table of Contents

Table of Contents

Epilogue

I adore the way
I know you adore me.

Dirty Sweet Poetry

Butterflies & Skin

Dirty Sweet Poetry

Tiffany Simone

Creative Talents Unleashed

The Good Kind

She's crazy love.

A lovely shade of crazy.

Crazy in the most beautiful way.

Only other beautifully crazy people,

can hold onto her type of

crazy love.

We Are

There is so much want and need,

tangled up in between...

We are sparklers.

We are lightening.

We are dreams.

Unstoppable

I don't chase. I won't.

Oh, but if you are all in,

I will fight.

We would be unstoppable,

because once you feel the power

of two people believing in love...

no longer will you settle for

good enough.

Wild

I want to be held captive in those arms,

caught,

caged by you,

the wild beast.

Hungry, you can lose yourself,

and do as you please.

Breathlessly I'll surrender,

laying down,

and giving you all of me.

Homecoming

Flesh against flesh,

I will be all the places

you've been waiting to collapse in.

There will be such beauty in the

homecoming of our skin.

Vow

I am your strength,

and only I make you weak.

It will be your blood that revives me,

only your mouth I seek.

We are more than words,

more than touch.

Two souls that collided

with a shocking rush.

Passion infused,

I gift you my trust.

Bound together,

forever,

this love.

LOVE For Me

LOVE, for me was a moment.

LOVE, was a voice that made my

heart race, a smile on a certain face

forever etched into my mind.

LOVE, for me will always taste a bit

like lime, feel like summer at night...

(add the twinkle lights),

a lap settled into just right,

and amber eyes a bit obsessed with

staring into mine.

LOVE, for me was a revelation,

and confessions,

and laughter,

and amazement...

full of thank you,

and undeniable chemistry,

and maybe we'll meet again

someday.

Problem Solver

I think the best way to solve

this problem is with

your mouth and handcuffs.

I'll yell when I'm better.

No Proof

To tell you the truth,

I don't think anyone can love me

as hard as I need,

or to the capacity as to which

I would love them.

Galaxy

Kiss me and get lost.

I am a galaxy of dreams,

your favorite wish come true,

guaranteed acceptance,

and everything that's love

to you.

Yellow Diamond

Barefoot and sun kissed,

all of the kids,

and some to witness

our day of combining hearts.

Ivory flowing gown, a bit of lace,

lots of skin, my hair down.

The darkness of your skin against

the sunlit glow,

I melt with each step,

those eyes I've grown to know.

Bleached sand dollars, dream catchers

and palm trees...

mix with the nights ahead of you plus me.

A yellow diamond, a gold band...

meaning more than jewelry upon our

hands.

Hands On

There is something

about the way

you never stop grabbing

for that space between my legs...

it cracks me up,

and turns me on,

all at once.

We seem to create an

inappropriate happiness,

in an all too serious world.

Proud

Love each other so blatantly obvious,

that the whole world can't help but

stare with shy smiles,

before looking away in amazement.

Evidence

She is evidence that there is

magic in this world...

that ONE.

She came around to show

you life through new eyes,

that wonders never cease,

and you are ready for

new things.

Fantasy

In my fantasies, the ones I've shared

with no one,

we are mutual intensity.

We are two bodies uniting, impossible to

let go.

We are best friends with restless hands.

We are love that everyone can visibly see.

We are primal with our needs and open,

pure vulnerability.

Mine and yours, raping each other to

claim more.

We'd apologize for the passion overtaking us.

Attack me with that kind of love.

Name

The desire is so strong.

I feel like I can taste it.

This ridiculous sense of want,

over something I've never had.

I'd like to name it after you.

The Team

I'm the Bonnie,

to his Clyde.

We knew we'd be trouble,

breaking the rules,

living the life.

Dare

He thought I had lost my edge.

I took it as a dare, and strapped on my

highest pair of stilettos and favorite dress

that left little to the imagination.

Walking past, dressed in sassy and sex,

I slowly batted long black lashes.

He looked uncomfortable.

"What?" I asked innocently, but not.

"You look...nice..." he replied.

"Huh, I'm going to go out and see if I

still have that 'edge' you were talking

about." I smiled, knowing I had everything inside

me I had always had. Time to let her out.

Firecracker

She's the kind of girl you don't let go of.

She's a firecracker that one,

a combination of a "Hell yes," and a "fuck no."

Hang on, because whatever it is,

you want it.

She's desire,

all love, passion and fire.

Same Dreams

You are my weakness,

my trigger,

the safe place inside my head.

You are my heartbeat,

my fountain wish,

the other side of my empty bed.

With the lights off,

and a bit of whiskey,

I let myself pretend it's you.

Arching my back,

giving into it,

knowing you have

the same dreams too.

For Me

I hope your words are always the sweetest

for me,

and your skin feels infinitely better,

simply by being next to mine.

Lingerie

She wears vulnerability

like lingerie...

all beautiful and exposed.

The problem is,

she really wants to take it off.

Butterflies & Skin

We are a mixture of protective arms,

and bite marks.

We are eye contact, and heavy breathing,

engaging conversations,

and the swirling of tongues.

We are fingers interlaced,

and the wetness between my

anxious legs.

I want to lay my naked body down,

and say this soul is for you.

We are butterflies and skin.

Falling

I'm flushed red with the sound of

your voice.

You go straight to my head,

making me drunk on this feeling.

High as the stars,

yet falling,

it's my heart that you're stealing.

She Is Water

She is water.

She will cleanse you,

give you an ocean of hope..

flowing consistent with her

love.

She is everything that is

beautiful.

Nothing could've ever

prepared you for the

shock of her touch,

or her release as she's

coming.

I Need You

I am much

too much

ME

to go through

this life alone.

I need a tear catcher,

a body to fall into,

and a love that rivals

my own.

Special

I will write you words

that no one else has read.

But first you must promise me

I will live in a

previously unowned

place in your head.

Worried

I can feel you fall away

and my entire body becomes tired with the fear of

where you are.

Maybe these are just quieter days,

or maybe you plan on running away

or maybe you think

I'm leaving you.

But I'm here.

I'm here and my face

is wet and

my hands are cold

and I use all my wishes

on hoping you want me like I want you.

Amazing

Put your hands here,

then here,

and here.

Learn me.

Bring me back to life.

I've forgotten what amazing

feels like.

Purple

I want colors.

I want fireworks,

and

someone missing me.

I want emotions so intense

I'm left with purple bruises

that don't make sense.

Thank You

All of a sudden there were words

I hadn't even asked for,

and I wanted to say,

"Thank you, thank you, thank you.."

with each sigh,

and 'I'm yours' became the look

in my eyes.

Sexy

She dresses in sexy words

because they feel good.

Don't misunderstand her though.

She wants the fairy tale ending,

hands longing for her,

eyes seeking out a certain shade

of green,

and a soul understanding exactly

what she means.

Nothing Less

Love me crazy.

Kiss me blind.

Tell me that I'm

One of a kind.

Cover me in big arms

I can trust.

Passion fueled,

let this devour us.

Stars

I kiss you because you were made for me.

I kiss you because of this discovery.

You are my light.

You've brought me home.

We kiss because

the stars told us so.

Need

The thought of your smile

being specifically for me...

makes me think

completely inappropriately.

You have become less

like a craving,

and more like a need.

Spaces

Everyone before you has carved out

little pieces of me.

Pieces, lessons, a part of my journey.

The spaces have left room for a

specific set of hands.

All that I am, now reserved

for one man.

Green

Her eyes were fucked up

shades of green;

kryptonite and jealousy.

Buckle up Baby,

This is the end of your

sanity.

Hypersensitive

Overloaded with a hypersensitivity

that feels like a death sentence,

she buzzes with vibrations

from other's electricity...

their feelings are breaking her alive.

Kindness is an absolute shock to

her system, but true love is the greatest wish

of her life.

On Fire

I don't know what you look

like,

standing beside or undressed

beneath me, but your words are the

right size for my body.

Your voice awakens insanity.

Get yourself ready,

you're what I desire.

When time falls away to

opportunity, we are going

to set this place on fire.

Before Moments

I want the "before" moments,

the looks,

the teasing,

the flirting,

the more.

I crave the intensity,

the mutual hunger,

knowing we aren't leaving alone.

I want to pull myself up to meet your mouth

in the middle of a crowded bar...

us both slightly hesitant,

but then almost taking it a bit too far.

I will lay down happily in your bed,

but the "before"

is what brings out the lioness

in my head.

Diamond

With her lover girl heart,

head full of dirty sweet wishes

and poet's mind,

you really should look closer.

That woman is a diamond

inside.

Mouth

I will never get tired of your kind words.

The more sincerity I hear from your mouth,

the more attention you'll get from mine.

Just Mine

He smelled like desire,

holding himself with confidence,

and I sensed protection.

Chemistry in our stomachs, and

hope in our bones.

Hands and hearts anxious,

never enough time...

and his eyes.

I wanted those on me

all the damn time.

Louder

I need a loud LOVE.

I need an auditorium microphone

cranked up to the highest it can go LOVE.

And if you can't be the one at the podium,

screaming this LOVE around...

you should step down,

and bow out

Sometimes Girl

I am not a SOMETIMES girl.

I don't want a SOMETIMES man.

I want hands at ALL the right times,

and hands at ALL the wrong.

I want deep kisses everyday, not

just when you want to play.

I want ALL that crazy electricity

lying just beneath our skin,

not SOMETIMES,

but ALL times, because I'm

not a SOMETIMES girl.

Every Little Thing

It's not just one thing.

It's everything.

It's nothing.

If we are going to do this,

it has to mean something.

It won't be one thing with me,

oh no, it will be every little thing.

It's everything or it's nothing.

Show Her

Wreck her body,

not her heart.

Devour each other

until there is nothing left.

Let love course through your veins,

as you move as one.

With each moan you're

explaining how insanely you

love her.

Sapiosexual

I do so many more tricks,

if you make love to my mind first.

She

She was a girl held together

by irrational hope and cheap glue.

She was prone to flights of fancy,

and more than her fair share of tears.

Too Much

I'm not a unicorn or a mermaid.

I'm the fog above the ocean,

a kitten you can cuddle with...

or a serpent,

with teeth.

Perfect

I want messy "just had sex hair."
I want my mouth swollen and my
chest flushed.
Let's be panting and sweaty,
with racing hearts.
All night we would attack
each other with love bites,
and randomly placed kisses.
We'd laugh and laugh,
at how wonderful this gift is.

Our Power

We are delusions of grandeur,

with greatness so grand...

an addiction to darkness,

and the darkness commands.

Love, fight for your happy

so your future shines bright.

You hold the power.

Let addiction breed light.

That Love

I think there might be a love out there

that very few of us know about...

A love that's more than comfort,

 or time,

or "we are fine."

I think there is a love out there that is

passion and obsession,

and, "I need you to breathe."

I think THAT is the love I need.

On The Edge

I'm caught on the edge of maybe,

of one day,

someday,

of soon.

Surrounded by the familiar,

with no way to get to the new.

Most of me wants to be stronger.

All of me seeks out sunlight.

None of me knows how to get there.

Hope spins with sadness each night.

Depth

Some words are so carefully crafted,

and yet full of absolutely nothing.

Depth is an illusion,

a romantic notion

I'm desperately trying

to hold on to.

Saying Goodbye

Exposing myself to you

and feeling you not even try...

everything is beautiful, but

you look like a lie.

When goodness finally arrives,

and acceptance comes my way,

stop, and put your head down.

You let a magic soul

go today.

Ironically

I'll probably be a bit difficult

for an undetermined,

possibly irrationally long

amount of time,

but I have to make sure

you really do love me.

I've lived without affection for so long,

and I'm all too aware

that words can mean nothing.

Teach Me

Teach me

how you go on each day.

Teach me

how you keep all these feelings at bay.

Teach me

because I feel my mind slipping away.

Beautiful

You are a sense of calm,

an endless sky

a brilliant sea.

You are the answer to all the questions.

You are a lover's eyes, and hope for destiny.

Poet Girl Addict

It's not going to be a choice

when you fall for me.

It's going to be a ridiculous accident,

that maybe you saw coming,

but didn't quite believe in right away.

Then, all of a sudden ...

you'd be swept up in green eyes,

and tornado love.

Like water after dehydration,

you wouldn't be able to get enough.

I'd be your worst vice and bad habit,

having you wanting,

and craving, a poet girl addict.

Grateful

I hope something feels lighter,

or happier,

or brighter inside today,

for absolutely no reason at all.

And you pause,

and say "thank you"

to the sky.

Fake

I write about love like it's a place I've been to.

Like when I was there,

I smiled and played.

I write like I slept in love forever.

I don't write like it was such a

brief stay.

Playing With Fire

We make heat with our eyes alone.

We are playing with fire,

but going slow.

Touching flames,

we burn our hands,

this love we finally understand.

Conforming

I will fold myself up

into tiny little pieces to

fit into your world

of acceptable emotions,

but please know I am

bursting at the seams

with demons to let go.

Mine

I want a man who admits I'm his weakness.

I want a song to bring us to our feet in the evening,

for no reason.

He'll kiss my hand and say,

"Baby, dance with me."

Someone who knows when the tears will fall,

so he stops the fight regardless of who is right or

wrong.

I want hands and possession,

and making out at a bar,

way past last call.

I want to see his eyes the moment he comes to

realize it's me. And I finally hear, "You're mine."

The Reason

In a world where I do often see gray,

you make me feel like colors.

You make me believe that I'm not broken.

You are the reason

beautiful words are spoken.

Gone

The second she knows she's a burden,

is the moment she'll hide her pain.

Hearing the sigh in your voice,

the walls start to call out her name.

Poison

You can actually feel her steal your

heart,

take control of your mind,

and simultaneously marry your

soul.

She's the best kind of poison.

Love Out Loud

Scream me to the world.

I'm exactly where you want to be.

Stake your claim and never ever take your hands off

me.

I want love notes and dirty jokes.

I want your hands always grabbing for my ass.

Loving through my sadness and smiling at my sass.

I want to be confident that whatever I put on,

you find me the most beautiful

woman you've ever known.

There is no second place. I'm the One.

My body would be your only home.

Fireworks would be our wedding song.

As a team, we could right every wrong.

Both of us happy and proud,

loving each other so loud.

Sassy Coated Sad

I'm a sassy attitude

that works really hard

to cover a soul

that's grown a little

too sad.

I wish you'd take the time

to look closer,

and know that none of

my sides are the hurtful

kind of bad.

Kind Eyes

I'm addicted to the way

your eyes keep telling me

I'm beautiful.

Dirty Sweet

Your sweetness leaves me weak,

probably because I know how dirty

your mind is underneath.

Our Dance

This life has a slow dance with our name on it.

A moment of time where you'll feel my breath

at the base of your neck,

and your hands will find themselves anxious

for moments that haven't even happened yet.

Another Time

Our words match.

Mouth echoing the goals

in our hearts.

That face of yours catches my

breath, and I feel you in all of

my parts.

You are a thousand butterflies,

a dream from another time.

Because

Because I like your face,

and your mind is dirty,

but your heart is sweet...

because tiptoe kisses are on my

list of my top five favorite things,

because what if it's incredible...

and we just need patience,

and shooting stars punching us

in the face.

Labels

There are the yelling kind,

the nagging kind,

the liars, and the cheaters...

the fake ones, bitches, girl haters,

and smile stealers.

Then, there is ME.

The here-is-my-heart,

ride or die,

loves faithfully,

and stays-on-your-mind

kind.

Sex & Candy

I hope he looks at me

with giant hearts in his eyes,

a craving for pure sugar,

and sex on his mind.

Favorite Color

He doesn't quite trust in the words,

because they have eaten him with lies.

But when he looks into her soul,

he admits his favorite color is

Green Eyes.

If

Only look at me like that

if you plan on

falling in love.

Underneath

It's not enough to just let

each other in.

I want us to crawl under

one another's skin,

make a home there...

and settle in.

Speaking Beautiful

Everything I say

becomes poetry

because my heart is

falling out

of my mouth.

Dear Heart

Dear Heart,

I will forever be a girl

in love with love,

and for that

I would like to thank you.

The always hopeful,

Dirty Sweet Poetry

Epilogue

Acknowledgements

I will never be able to express my gratitude enough, but I do need to acknowledge the following... First, I need to thank all the beautiful souls that are genuine lovers of words and art of all kinds. Those that have been following me as "Dirty Sweet Poetry" on social media since 2014 have given me a strength in myself that I forgot I possessed.

Thank you to my amazing children, who are so good for letting Mommy write…and sitting next to me becoming future artists all their own.

I'm blessed for my forever friends Tricia and Amanda, who are the kind of people you know will always stay. Hugs and swear words to Gia. Two years isn't that long right? A special thank you to cover artist Mitch Green for making my request for "something pretty" come true.

This book would literally not exist without help from the unbelievable writer and beautiful soul Sarah Lamar King. Sarah guided me through the entire process…basically dumbing everything down for me. I am forever indebted to her.

Also, thank you to my wonderful siblings… especially Tyler, for "getting it," and helping me breathe when I hyperventilate in parking lots. And to Eric, thank you for being my family.

Dad…look I'm smarter than we thought.

Tiffany Simone

About the Author

Tiffany Simone is a Chicago based author and the divorced mother of two beautiful and creative children. She has been writing primarily on social media since 2014, where she creates her unique blend of sexual sweetness as *Dirty Sweet Poetry*.

Tiffany has amassed a large following, and now brings that same passion for sensuality and love to her first book, *'Butterflies and Skin'*. Tiffany hopes to grow and evolve in her love, and her writing, while passionately pursuing her own Dirty and Sweet storybook ending.

- John Hunley

Visit Tiffany's Author Page At:

www.ctupublishinggroup.com/tiffany-simone-.html

About the Book

'Butterflies and Skin' is an invitation to a journey of sensuality, sultry and tactile pleasure. A wonderful collection of short prosy and poetic pieces; *Tiffany Simone* speaks with raw honesty, unabashedly about her desire for love, her longings, her losses and painful path to finding herself.

This book is written for true romantics, who relish in the truth of laying themselves bare while in the pursuit of love. There are moments of lyrical melancholy; there are also moments of pure fire lit passion, delighting in carnal pleasure, without apology.

For anyone who has ever been hopelessly in love, has ever lost in love or reawakened by a new love, this is a book the reader will identify with. Simone speaks with clarity, giving voice to our hidden thoughts of decadent pleasures.

A beautiful read to evoking secret passions…

- Brenda-Lee Ranta, author of *Myriad of Perceptions*

Creative Talents Unleashed

www.ctupublishinggroup.com

Creative Talents Unleashed is an independent publishing group that offers writers an opportunity to share their writing talents with the world. We are committed to fostering and honoring the work of writers of all cultures.

For More Information Contact:

info@ctupublishinggroup.com